Anonymus

Henrietta

A true story

Anonymus

Henrietta
A true story

ISBN/EAN: 9783741112744

Manufactured in Europe, USA, Canada, Australia, Japa

Cover: Foto ©Andreas Hilbeck / pixelio.de

Manufactured and distributed by brebook publishing software (www.brebook.com)

Anonymus

Henrietta

HENRIETTA.

A TRUE STORY.

NEW YORK:
P. O'SHEA, 104 BLEECKER STREET.
1863.

HENRIETTA.

A TRUE STORY.

I.

A SPOILED CHILD.

It was a fine morning in spring. The sun half hidden beneath a cloud of vapor, cast its pale rays on the green meadows of Beance, and on its fields enamelled with daisies, and buttercups; a gentle fresh breeze balanced the flexible stems of the dandelion, and scattered those little downy leaves, which in your simple and expressive language you call candles (chandelles). The steeples of the neighboring churches detached themselves, as it were, from the blue background, and all nature awoke, smiling and adorned.

A little girl sitting amidst the wild and aromatic plants, strewed flowers around her, and sung to the murmur of the pure and crystal-like undulations of a stream that flowed at her feet. Concealed in the foliage of the neighboring oak trees, the linnet and the lark seemed joyous to accompany her notes.

"Henrietta, look how pretty they are!" exclaimed another little girl, as loud as she could make herself be heard from a distance, and running out of breath up to her young com panion, she threw herself down beside the latter on the green sward.

"Look at their golden wings," added she, showing Henrietta the bright butterflies that fluttered in her gauze net. "Oh, I am so overjoyed to have found such beauties—this last hour I have been chasing them around the meadows and the wild-brier hedges."

"You can talk on, Antoinette," answered Henrietta, "they are nothing to mine."

"Oh! as to that, you mistake; if they are not more beautiful, they are at least as beautiful: confess it."

"Indeed, no, Miss, I prefer mine; they are larger, and they are better shaded; mine are of every color. Go and ask Miss Gertrude. I am sure she will say I am right."

"Well, be it so, I shall be satisfied with whatever she will say; let me then help you to fill your basket with your flowers—it will be done sooner." And the obliging little girl stooped to pick up the flowers, but Henrietta plucked them impatiently away from her hands.

"No, you shall not," screamed she—"you shall not; you spoil them. I can do without your help, Miss— you did not help me to gather them, so . . . And putting them pell-mell into the basket, she tried to carry them home; but the handles slipped from her little hands, and the flowers fell on the grass. Antoinette offered again her services; Henrietta refused them sulkily, and fastening a ribbon to her basket, drew them along, quite proud of the invention; and though the burden was not heavy, it was awkward for a little girl who was accustomed to be waited upon. Antoinette, carrying her basket on her shoulder, gayly tripped on before her friend.

"Don't go so fast," screamed Henrietta, "I shall not stay behind. I wish to be at the house as soon as you. See how far you are from me." And she strove to run, but seeing that all her flowers, which she shook so violently, were scattered on the ground, she began to cry, and remained on the way. Antoinette, quite in despair about her little friend, and well aware of her obstinacy, ran to fetch Henrietta's mother, and told her what had happened, without adding any malignant reflections. When Madame D'Heronville saw her child in tears, she took her in her arms and loaded her with kisses, gave her sweetmeats, and instead of chiding her for her obstinacy, she listened with pernicious indulgence, to the little head-strong child who screamed with sobs: "Mamma, Antoinette ran before me, and she is the cause of my basket falling; she is forever teasing me."

Antoinette was at one of the windows of the house; she was seen through the honeysuckle and the creeping vines that climbed the walls and diffused a soft somber shade through the room, she showed her pretty fair head, and playing with the flowers that were interwoven in the insterstices of the balcony.

"Go away from there, Antoinette," said Henrietta, "you are breaking all the branches of my vines; don't you hear me, you are bruising my honey-suckles! there are some scattered on the ground." The amiable little Antoinette withdrew without answering, though she was the elder. Henrietta was only five, but she felt that one could not expect reason from a child whose every caprice was law for her weak parents.

Henrietta was the only child of a

rich nobleman, who lived in the environs of Chartres. Her rare beauty had rendered her so vain that even at so early an age she was one of the most imperious and troublesome of children. Every thing should give way to her will, and unfortunately for her, her father and mother, who idolized her, forgot in their deluded tenderness the future they prepared for their child; they only thought of the present moment, as if she were destined to live forever under the paternal wing, that they would vainly spread so as to protect her from the slightest blast, the slightest damp. They made of her a pretty doll unable to endure, without complaining, the cold of winter and the heat of summer; undoubtedly she was, in the midst of all her apparent happiness, more to be pitied than any of her companions.

A few days after this scene, Madame D'Heronville was working at one of the windows, when her daughter entered sobbing.

"Gracious!" exclaimed the mother with emotion, for she could not bear to see her child in tears, "what has happened? what is the matter, my love; did you fall?"

"Mamma, I begged of Jack to go to the fair to buy me some gingerbread and other cakes; he will not, he refused!"

"Why will he not go? He must have given you some reason."

"He says that papa ordered him to go in another direction. He seemed to laugh at my tears. He is a boor—he is impertinent—he ought to be sent away."

"But, my angel, if your papa wishes him to go elsewhere, he must obey."

"He can do the two errands at the same time, and I must have gingerbread; you promised me some this morning after my music lesson."

"Henrietta, I beg you to be more reasonable. I shall send the man to get some cakes, but not at the fair, he has no time to spare."

"I must have cakes from the fair; the others are not so good; they are hard."

"Why, those of the fair are the same; they are bought here."

"I don't care, Jack shall not laugh at me. I told him to go and buy me some at the fair, and he must go to the fair; otherwise he will gain over me, and another time he would not listen to me."

And she began to sob violently. In vain did her mother beg of her to cease. She persisted in her resolution, and it was decided that the errand was to be put off until night, and that Jack should start after dinner. Henrietta had a thousand other whims, and as she was not hungry when the servant returned, and besides that she no longer cared for the cakes, she said that they were not good; that Jack had deceived her by not buying them at the fair. Then she asked for tea and bread, and so tormented her too indulgent mother, who now refused to satisfy her whims. The little self-willed creature then became so angry that she threw the cakes out of the window. A little chimney sweeper, who was eating, with good appetite, a piece of dry bread at Madame D'Heronville's door, picked the cakes up, and feeling quite glad at the windfall, and devouring them with his eyes, thanked Henrietta for what he got. When the spoiled child saw them in another's possession, she began to cry, saying they prevented her eating them, so as the little chimney sweeper, who was there waiting, could have them. Thus she went through a thousand absurd and different caprices. She wanted Miss Gertrude to return and buy her some more gingerbread, but her father forbade it, because this scene had gone too far, and he began also to perceive that his daughter's faults were increasing every day.

Thus did Henrietta spend her time, abusing the influence she had over her parents. Her success in dancing and music made her extremely vain. She was learning those arts when she was learning to read. She executed wonders on the harpsichord, but she was ignorant of all other things in which a young lady should be a proficient.

Nature had endowed her with a great talent for music, and we will see that at the age of nine, she became the delight of all the great ladies of the capital, and gained favor at Court for her musical acquirements.

Those triumphs afforded her many joyous moments, yet in the course of time, they were no longer a source of honor or happiness; she reaped but little benefit, for she lacked many essential qualities.

II.

A CONCERT AT COURT.

HAVING become famed for her precocious talent, Henrietta was invited to the Court. She was smiling complacently and contemplating her festive dress, so fresh and so dazzling; she thought of the triumphal entry she would make into the royal rooms, and her heart leaped with impatience and pleasure when she dreamed of the joyous day—of that morrow so desired, so long wished for; how she longed for the time to elapse; she would have given all her childhood's years for one instant, for that instant which would make an epoch in her life, and leave her sweet and flattering recollections. With less levity and less frivolity, she would have regretted the beautiful past, when so young, she was surrounded by her tender parents, she had a friendly hand to guide her and to dry her tears. A day will come when she will appreciate it; she will know that a mother replaces every thing, but her nothing can replace.

The morrow came; several hours were devoted to her toilet.

The vain Henrietta stood before her glass of brilliant crystal and performed a thousand prim and affected airs, which were, she thought, to secure her the conquest of all the choice company of the Court; then she decked herself out with her necklace and her flowers, which she placed and replaced in a hundred various ways. She never tired admiring them, for they were a new and complete set that had been bought for her that day. Her mother's maid powdered her hair, applied rouge to her cheeks, and put on beauty-patches, fastened her frills and put on her dress,—for such was the fashion of the XVIIIth century,—and when her mother had given a last glance at her daughter's toilet, they entered a carriage that took them to Versailles, where the Court then was.

On the way, Henrietta begged of

her mother to lower the windows, so that they could see her thus decked and adorned, and the mother, who was proud of her child's beauty, did not refuse to satisfy this foolish whim. Maternal tenderness served, perhaps, as an excuse for Madame D'Heronville, who otherwise had many good qualities.

When the mother and the daughter entered the concert-room, one of the greatest artists of the day was executing on the harpsichord a brilliant piece which captivated the attention of the whole assembly, but when Madame and Miss D'Heronville were announced, they exclaimed, on all sides: " Charming, sweet, *angelical*."

Henrietta blushed with pleasure,

for she knew that this praise was for her. The Queen* placed her beside her, and said in the most amiable and gracious manner, that she would be delighted to hear her perform, that her fame had already reached the Court. Reassured by this mark of interest, the young lady advanced to the instrument with firm confidence. Many persons regretted that she did not have that air of modesty that adds lustre to merit; from thence they conceived for her an unfavorable opinion; others thought it might be the effort of her youthfulness, and they excused her in consideration of her talent.

She preludes cleverly; her tones,

* Mary Leckinska, wife of Louis XV.

at first, soft and sweet, sad and tender, dispose the soul to deep emotion; her fingers glide nimbly and skilfully over the keys that she sounds with admirable dexterity. But, no longer is it the melancholy lament of an old ballad that is heard from afar; nor is it the melodiousness and imitative sigh of the night-wind that re-echoes through the gale; they are joyous brilliant strains, rich with expression and fancy. Suddenly, Henrietta closes her music, and yields to her own inspirations. Then it is the inhabitant of Switzerland who sadly leaves his cottage home, and who is roused from his dreams and souvenirs by the sound of the war-trumpet; or it is the lament of the orphan and

the return of the exile to his country.
Above all, it is the voice of the heart
that Henrietta seems to render so
truly, for genius inspires her! . . . .
Alas! why has a vicious education
suppressed the feelings that are alone
manifested in her music!

The audience is enraptured, enchanted, ravished; they applaud with
enthusiasm, and a shower of sugarplums and flowers cover the little
prodigy; who really believes herself
a privileged being; they assail her,
they surround her, they load her
with caresses and compliments, they
dispute to have her on their knees.
The Queen and the ladies of honor
even congratulate the mother, who
is elated; the princesses embrace

in their beautiful arms, the little girl, who is like one encircled in a wreath of roses. Poor Henrietta was charmed. This triumph, this luxury, this room glittering with light, that undulating drapery of velvet, and above all, those women, whose diamonds in their dazzling effulgence rivaled even the chandeliers suspended from the ceiling; those lovely women, who loaded her with kisses and praise, all seemed to contribute to intoxicate her, and her vanity was at its utmost height.

III.

THE COMPANION OF HER CHILDHOOD.

A few days afterwards, Antoinette came to compliment Henrietta for the success she had obtained; the latter received her with an air of protection, for she was happy to recount to her young friend, the incidents of that memorable evening; she showed her also, the *Mercury of France*, the paper in which the following article was inserted:

"Yesterday, appeared at the Court concert, Miss Henrietta D'Heronville, a young lady, aged nine years, who executed several pieces on the harpsichord. Her brilliant performance, the flexibility of her fingers, every thing augurs that she will one day rival the greatest artists of the Capital—she may even surpass them. . . . . She obtained the approbation of all, and we are happy to pay a tribute to her rare and precocious talents."

The good and candid Antoinette participated in the happiness of her friend, and neither jealousy nor envy entered her heart. But Henrietta continued:

"What a pity that you have not some particular talent! What have your parents been thinking of? They bring you up as a poor girl; now you might turn it to account. My poor Antoinette, I could not take you to the Court with me; besides, with your mean clothes, they would say you were my maid. They would say that your mother does not care for you. Oh, surely she is not as good as mine, who is always happy to see me dressed and adorned. I remember, too, that your mother is very severe with you; she never yields to your wishes."

"Henrietta," answered Antoinette, who was pained and grieved, "you hurt me when you accuse my parents for their want of tenderness; they have not neglected my education; on the contrary, they have constantly cared for it. Severer, but as tender as yours, my mother wishes me to be a domesticated woman, a woman skilled in the duties of a housewife. She thinks it useless to sacrifice so many years to frivolous pursuits that we abandon later, for instance when we are married. She teaches me grammar, history, geography. She gives me little stories to copy; this amuses me more than any thing else. She tells me often that in study there is less excitement than in worldly enjoyments, but that it is sweeter and more lasting—enjoyments, in fact, that leave no regrets. I should be delighted to have, like you, some extraordinary talent, but this is a gift that nature does not bestow upon every one, and for which, besides, mamma would not have sacrificed every thing.

Indeed, if I had the choice of frivolous pleasures and my own dear occupations, I should not wish to change."

In her turn, the proud Henrietta felt mortified. She had never taken the trouble to study any other lessons but her music. She could not write a word of orthography, and if you had assured her that Pontoise was the capital of France, she would have believed your word.

"Ah! indeed," replied she, with humor, "what would you want me to do with such troublesome science? Have I not to practice, my friend? Besides, I have no desire to be a pedant. We shall see which of us two will succeed the better. It is most probable that you will never be presented at Court."

And with a saucy air she began to prelude upon her harpsichord without paying any further attention to poor Antoinette, who, perceiving herself thus disdained, left with a bursting heart, and her eyes full of tears. In spite of her gentle disposition, it was a long while before she returned to see Henrietta.

IV.

ITALY.

The Queen had presented Henrietta with a complete outfit, splendid dresses, a harpsichord, enriched with beautiful and graceful paintings, and a pension of five hundred francs, to be drawn from her private purse. She likewise expressed the desire that the young musician should go to Italy, hoping that a sojourn in the country of fine arts would perfect her accomplishments, and place her on a par with the illustrious artists of her reign. Proud of the royal favor, Henrietta was enchanted at the thoughts of a voyage that appeared as one continued triumphal march. Everywhere she seemed to gather an ample harvest of wreaths, and on her way the child saw but the roses, her mother casting carefully aside the thorns. Therefore she was without buckler against the trials that awaited her through life.

We shall allow a few years to elapse, years that offer few interesting occurrences, and the details of which would be monotonous. We shall accompany Henrietta under the pure sky of Italy, that sky that inspires poets, painters, and musicians· Perhaps your young fancy has already carried you to that beautiful country, where there are so many magnificent monuments raised to the memory of great men, and you have envied the fate of our heroine contemplating the ruins of Rome, and visiting the delightful kingdom of Naples. Follow my bark, and let us glide gently on the clear blue undulations of the lake of Agnano, which flows in the environs of the same city. Its waves are so gentle that you would suppose them to repose. The evening is lovely, full of that calm serenity of an Italian climate; the air is pure and perfumed; the sun is setting, and reflects its rays on the transparent water, the surface of which is disturbed an instant by the old boatman's oar; his arms were stripped and nervous, and he sang a *canzonetta*, that was listened to by four women sitting in the pretty gondola. The two elder ones had a noble respectable appearance, the other two were young girls, white and roseate; they appeared to enjoy the brilliant sight that was presented to their view, for they were at an age when impressions are as sudden as transient. One of them is handsome, her eyes are black and beautiful, her fine silky hair falls on her shoulders, and encloses one of the most exquisite of faces, her figure is slight and slender, her attire elegant and rich. But this girl, so aerial, so fair, this girl who fascinates and bewitches you, is a perfidious syren; she speaks words, but they come not from the heart; her coral lips utter expressions of bitterness and scorn; forever preoccupied about her own person, she studies no one's happiness, and her ivory brow contracts at the slightest contradiction. You have recognized her: it is Henrietta. The other has less brilliancy, but what expressive features! what grace and simplicity in her appearance! what modesty and kindness in her countenance, where the candor of a pure soul is strongly depicted; her smile wins every heart; though she utter not a word, you already love her; her goodness is a gift from heaven, but her reason has been formed and developed by the influence of a sound education. It is Antoinette, the com panion of Henrietta's childhood. She is closely seated by her sick mother, upon whom the air of Italy has already effected some change. Angel of virtue and of devotedness, she has not gone thither for triumph nor amusements, but for the climate which she hopes may have some influence on her beloved mother's health. Her tenderness, her care, her patience are inexhaustible; filial love can go no further; nevertheless she thinks she has never done enough, and in her humility she prays unceasingly to God to bestow upon her new virtues.

The sun disappears behind the trees at the water's edge; its rays penetrate through those high poplars that border the lake, as a green sash; they cover them with gold and purple clouds, which resemble globes of fire flying in the atmosphere; smooth, bright streams shine radiantly in the heavens like millions of rubies and topazes. At this solemn moment the soul is penetrated with respect and admiration; you incline before the fading day as a few hours before you welcomed the awaking of nature. Night casts its mysterious veil on the lake : the landscape presents another aspect; fleeting shades gleam afar; the gondolier's song is lower, it seems to invite to sleep: every thing announces the hour of rest. The bark stops at the shore. Antoinette gives her arm to her mother, whom she carefully wraps in a silken pelisse, fearing for her the night breeze that cools others.

On the other hand, Henrietta attends a concert, where she shines and reaps new success. Thus did each of them follow their destiny—one the idol of the public, the other the guardian angel of her mother.

V.

TWO MARRIAGES.

ANTOINETTE, as we have said, had been obliged to leave France, the climate of Italy being more suitable to her mother's delicate constitution; the doctors having likewise given their opinion that a severer climate might cause the death of her beloved mother. She sacrificed all; she bid farewell to her own fair France, but she kept her childhood's recollections to recall those happy hours. She always fancied herself in the meadows, amongst the flowers and the lambs, treading in her girlish wanderings the green grass, studded with blue flowers and daisies; happy, then, when she entered the house with a rich provision of strawberries and nuts, or laden with branches of hawthorn that perfumed the air. That age of innocence and of simple pleasures has fled, and other years have brought on duties and sorrows; but Antoinette can yet enjoy some satisfaction, for her heart is satisfied, and her conscience reproaches her not.

She is going to marry a young Italian, who has learned to appreciate her sense and her rare qualities; their union takes place under the most happy auspices; we shall soon see her enjoying a fortune that she has doubled by her economy and her activity, and dividing her time between her husband and her mother, who repay her in love and in gratitude.

One year after, the orange blossoms quivered on Henrietta's breast; the folds of a long lace veil floated over her shoulders; her brilliant dress, the sumptuous equipage that conducted her to the altar, the rich livery of the lackeys, every thing bespoke pomp and opulence; Henrietta was at the height of her ambition.

Then it was a succession of festivities and amusements, where the young musician displayed a luxury, little in harmony with her revenues; on this score she had also sacrificed to her vanity, for the young man she married was of noble family but poor. She had contracted habits of indolence and of dissipation which led her to neglect music, and to spend a great deal of her fortune.

Each day brought new fancies, that should be satisfied, no matter at what price.

Her husband, who had been captivated by her admirable talent, soon regretted that he had united his fate with that of a woman, who had so many vices without one good quality. Henrietta's caprice, her passionate temper, her egotism and her whims, destroyed whatever feeling he had had for her, and a separation appeared to him to be the only means of obtaining peace; moreover, the dissipated life that this imprudent young woman led, shattered her health and withered her beauty; therefore, she had no longer enough charms left to secure the heart of a man who had been a moment dazzled by her outward advantages. But let us not pity her, her mother is yet with her.

VI.

MISERY AND ABANDONMENT.

In a room where misery and disorder prevail, but where there are yet a few remains of past opulence, is a woman reclining in an arm chair; her face is thin and altered; and were there any signs of resignation in her countenance, you would feel an interest in her behalf; but instead, you read an expression of grief and discouragement; her contracted lips, the lines that mark her forehead, betray an irritability and an impatience, which are not the characteristics of sorrow, nevertheless a great grief overwhelms her. . . . She is now alone; her mother, her good mother is now no longer there to watch over her beloved daughter, in whom she scarcely saw a fault. Madame D'Heronville has fallen a victim to the misfortunes of her daughter; she was unprepared for such trials, and Henrietta now feels the affliction and the want of her mother. Oh! yes, she has fathomed the depth of her loss; she realizes it to its full extent. Poor in virtue, poor in love, aud poor in income! . . . . Her sickness has obliged her to abandon her music, which might have been some resource; her debts have absorbed the little she had remaining; her jewelry, her trinkets, her diamonds are sold, and soon . . . . Oh! how she suffers, for she is struggling against pride and misery, and she has concealed her position from every one. Her husband has left Italy, feeling the greatest indifference for one who had formerly been his companion.

But Antoinette has sought her; at length she has discovered where her childhood's companion lives; she hastens, she flies to the spot, and speaking to her with those touching words that come from the heart, she desires her to follow her, where she can enjoy the care of friendship and the comforts of wealth, to which she has been so much accustomed.

"I wish to see you every day, my dear Henrietta," said she; "and I cannot leave my husband and my children. Come, then, with us, I want a sister, you know I always wished to have one; come, you will be that sister."

Henrietta extended her thin hand, and grateful, repentant tears dropped from her eyes; for in her days of prosperity, she had shunned the company of Antoinette, whose plain and humble tastes found no sympathy with her. This generous friend had already forgotten Henrietta's faults, and she strove to afford her some consolation in her latter days. She leaned her upon her arm and took her out to walk in the country where she could enjoy the mild influence of spring; when seated in her armchair, Antoinette would read to her aloud, presenting to her the most smiling pictures, and affording her agreeable amusement to banish regrets and the bitter thoughts that absorbed her. Thus she persisted till she brought a smile upon the lips of the sick woman, and a calm to that heart consumed with repentance. She watched and prayed unceasingly at her pillow, and if it were not in her power to prolong her existence, she at least soothed her in her last moments. Henrietta died of consumption in the arms of Antoinette, calling down blessings upon her and her family.

GRETCHEN;

OR,

The Chapel of Winkelried.

NEW YORK:
P. O'SHEA, 104 BLEECKER STREET.
1863.

Entered according to Act of Congress, in the year 1868, by

P. O'SHEA,

In the Clerk's Office of the District Court of the United States, for the Southern District of New York.

C. A. ALVORD, STEREOTYPER AND PRINTER.

GRETCHEN;

OR,

THE CHAPEL OF WINKELRIED.

On the outskirts of Stanz, in a pleasant Swiss cottage, a family of Unterwald was assembled one winter's evening around a bright fire. Whilst the mother and her two daughters were busily arranging linen work, the father and his elder son, each a knife in hand, were cutting with wonderful skill and admirable patience, those charming little nicknacks which are sent to other countries, where they are sold for their weight in gold—diminutive cottages, dancing-bears, whistles, figured paper knives, cases representing fishes, &c. It was not as tradesmen that Peter Wurmser and Heinrich worked: there was emulation between them; and Peter was pleased with his pupil. He therefore spoke approvingly.

"Well done, my boy," said he, "well done! you are getting along. You are but fifteen, and can earn already your own living, if your parents were to die."

"Oh, dear father," cried Heinrich, dropping his work, and dashing away a tear, "don't speak so. I separated from you! oh, no, impossible; I could not live: we are so happy together."

In his turn, Peter was moved; he shook his head, and said with emotion: "Rest assured I have no intention to make you grieve. See, the attitude of that bear clinging to the tree is not quite natural; improve the left paw and trace out the claws distinctly. . . . . " John," continued he, changing his tone and his countenance, and addressing his second son, who was standing by the fire, and whose ironical smile was ill-suppressed, "why do you smile? do you imagine that you are somebody because you are doing nothing? If you had not been so headstrong as to persist in not learning our trade, you now might be useful, both to yourself and to others; instead of this, you run wild through the mountains like a chamois."

Without appearing much impressed by the rebuke, John answered: "I ask your pardon, dear father, I did not wish to pain you. . . . I did not intend it."

"What pains me is your indolence."

"Let not this trouble you; I am now fourteen; I shall soon be of age, to shoulder a gun and volunteer."

His mother shuddered; Peter struck sharply on the table the handle of his knife, and exclaimed: "More of your foolish notions, unhappy boy! Listen: what I am now going to say, regards your future peace and happiness; and mind—though you are a source of great anxiety to your mother and me, I love you because you are my son, and that you are not bad at heart. But why fill your head with ideas of war and epaulettes? At your age war is a fine thing; your dreams are full of the smoke of battlefields. . . . At mine, one realizes—one sees clearly, what is the true value of military glory. Out of so many fine young fellows, who leave with their guns upon their shoulders, following the flag and shouting patriotic airs, how many of them return after a few years, when the cannon will have decimated their ranks? Not one half. Slight motives are the cause of bloody massacres. Believe me, John, you are making a bad choice, and a time will come when it will be known to its full extent.

"However, father"———

"There is no however. If you wish facts, I'll give them to you. I, an old campaigner, I who have armed myself for the defence of my country, and who have longed many and many a time for peace and tranquillity. Here, without going very far, the history of this canton will furnish a most convincing proof of the desolation of war.

"Oh, tell us, father," said they unanimously.

"With all my heart, my children," answered Peter Wurmser.

"It was in 1798. You were then

with the angels, my children, and you, Prettle, my wife, you were no higher than my boot. I was then a robust lad, and I was witness of what I am about relating.

"On a fine autumn day, Master Herman, a rich man of this part of the country, was wedding his charming daughter, Gretchen, to one of our finest young fellows, Fredcrick, the best marksman of his time. What a handsome couple they were! the one sixteen, the other twenty; both comely, both favored by fortune. The whole canton resounded with shouts of joy and acclamation; all the bells of Stanz rang forth a merry chime, and the house of the bride was hung with verdure. Music accompanied them on their way to church, and the peals of the *vivats* were deafening. However, Frederick's countenance had a certain impress of sadness, and in vain did he endeavor to smile. This painful preoccupation did not escape Gretchen.

"'My dear,' said she, in a low voice, 'what is the matter? I beseech you to tell me.'

"'Me? . . Nothing,' . . . stammered Frederick.

"Gretchen loved him much, and insisted, with such tender entreaties, that at length he answered:

"'How can my heart be light and gay when our country's liberty is threatened! The French Directory has spread its armies throughout

Switzerland, to break up our old confederation; blood flows at Berne; at Lucerne, and elsewhere there have been unfortunate engagements. You are aware that the troops of General Schonenbourg have attacked our canton three times.'

" ' But three times they have been repulsed,' answered the young bride.

" ' Defeat provokes persistance,' replied Frederick, ' and humiliation is the mother of fury. The French will return.'

" Before Gretchen, whose demeanor expressed intense emotion, could answer, Herman, annoyed at this mysterious conversation, stepped forward and said: ' My children, you have no right to speak together. Moreover, what means this gloom? Now, then, be cheerful—zounds! . . . . . . here we are at the church.'

"This was a solemn moment; the porch was wide open; before the altar, adorned with flowers, stood a venerable priest; the fiddlers from without were playing lively airs, whilst within a musician performed on the harpsichord. The bride and bridegroom knelt down, the crowd followed their example, and the ceremony commenced. But Frederick was not the only one in Unterwald whose mind was troubled; many a one present turned his head and gazed earnestly towards the door. . . Suddenly Gretchen started up and shuddered; guns were heard at a distance from the village. And instantly a man who had ascended into the steeple rushed down, crying: 'Here is the enemy!'"

"The sounds grew distinct. Arrived unawares at Stanzstadt, the French had driven back the foot soldiers of Unterwald. Fire and sword marked their passage; even the square on which stood the church, had become the scene of a furious combat. Balls were fired through the windows, and the chapel was vacated by the terrified crowd. Frederick remained cool in the face of this danger; he turned to his beloved and said: 'The ceremony must be concluded. Kneel, Gretchen, kneel!'

"Then he said to the priest, 'Father, give us your blessing.' But the priest, leaning against the altar, did not answer, a ball had entered his heart. . . . He was dead! A heavenly serenity was spread over the features of the venerable old man.

"A mountaineer rushed in, thrilled with horror and stained with blood.

"'Frederick,' cried he, 'stay no longer here; your place is in our ranks; our leaders have fallen—replace them.'

"'I am at your service,' answered the young man, resolutely, 'but what news? Is Sarnen attacked?'

"'Sarnen is attacked. They are yet safe in the chapel of St. Jacques.'

"'And the chapel of Winkelried?'

"'It is full of ammunition, but it has no one to defend it.'

"'To defend it!' repeated Gretchen, 'the chapel must be protected, and if there be not enough men, the women will replace them!'

"'What say you,' cried Frederick, in a tender and melancholy tone, 'you fight! You, so delicate, so frail, to imperil your life! Leave to others such dreadful strife, and return to your father's house.'

"'No,' answered she; 'the moment of timidity and weakness is passed. I feel strong all at once. Do not try to dissuade me; my will is as firm as the basis of our mountains. Fly to your post—I to mine.'

"'A parting farewell, then, my

dear Gretchen,' murmured Frederick. 'Let us hope to meet in a better world, since we part at the foot of our holy altar.'

"'Yes, there we shall meet,' said she exultingly, 'there our trials will be ended; there we shall enjoy happiness pure and unalloyed. Farewell! Farewell!' ..

"Whilst Frederick rejoined his companions in arms, Gretchen, followed by seventeen intrepid daughters of Switzerland, passed from the church, by a side door, and hastened to take possession of the little fortress.

"The chapel of Winkelried was an edifice of medium size, solidly built, roofed with red tiles, and protected by iron railed loop-holes. Its name originated, most likely, from Arnold of Winkelried, who immortalized himself by his sublime devotedness at the battle of Sempach. The chapel was well filled with provisions, as the mountaineer had so announced; moreover, to intercept the roads leading thereto, large trunks of trees and enormous blocks of rocks barricaded their entries. Therefore, it was not difficult to defend this post.

"Gretchen hoped to keep back the enemy so as to allow the inhabitants of the neighboring villages time to reinforce their brothers of Unterwald.

"Meanwhile the mountains re-echoed the discharge of the musketry

—every spot presented a vast battlefield; the valleys, the villages, and even the houses. If the attack was furious, the resistance was firm; for the French, it was in view of military glory; for the Swiss, it was life or liberty. The distance of the road made Gretchen suppose, for a moment, that her compatriots had repulsed the enemy, but this illusion was dissipated at the sight of foreign soldiers, who appeared in the depth of the valley, with their drums beating and their flags unfurled. The brave girls embraced each other, and swore to die for liberty. When the soldiers approached without mistrust, Gretchen fired from the chapel: the ball of her rifle mortally wounded one of the officers; her companions followed her example, and the carnage caused by their firing was but too great a proof of their correct aim. The French were unsheltered, and in the midst of the deadly projectiles showered upon them, whilst those young heroines were protected by their ramparts of stone and iron. Notwithstanding the victims who were shot down on all sides, those men were too brave to abandon their post; they would sooner have died on the spot. Dashing, then, across the obstacles which lay in their way, they advanced near enough to the chapel to return the fire of their adversaries. Yet the smoke prevented them from seeing their enemies. The greater number of Gretchen's companions had either fallen dead or wounded. Those who were unable to fight, charged the arms, and thus made themselves useful. At length came the moment when all resistance was fruitless.

"'Surrender!' cried the French.

"Gretchen cast a look upon the horizon, and there from a building, she saw floating the colors of the enemy.

"All was over.

"'Surrender!' repeated the soldiers.

"But the poor girl did not answer; she was in prayer. At that same moment, a spark falling into a barrel of powder, spread fire throughout the building. It was a horrible explosion, and the chapel of Winkelried was in flames. One would have thought it an earthquake or the eruption of a volcano.

"The first soldiers who entered the ruins, dropped to the ground with fright, on discovering that their formidable adversaries were women. They went away with sorrowful hearts, cursing the while the sad necessity of war.

"Well," said master Peter, as he ended the narrative and relighted his pipe, "well, John, do you still think that the condition of soldier is the finest in the world? And that the vain satisfaction of shouldering a gun, replaces that of a family and home? Does not the narrative I have given you, show the deplorable consequences of those struggles where force and number triumph so often over right and justice?"

John drew softly nigh his father, his countenance impressed with deep emotion, and tears in his eyes, and clasping respectfully the old man's hands, said: "Believe me, father, to-morrow I shall go to our neighbor Simon Frantz, the farmer, and you will see that your son can become a good husbandman."

www.ingramcontent.com/pod-product-compliance
Lightning Source LLC
Chambersburg PA
CBHW020245090426
42735CB00010B/1843